Welcoming the Light

Welcoming the Light

Services for Advent to Candlemas

David Adam

kevin mayhew

kevin
mayhew

First published in Great Britain in 2009 by Kevin Mayhew Ltd
Buxhall, Stowmarket, Suffolk IP14 3BW
Tel: +44 (0) 1449 737978 Fax: +44 (0) 1449 737834
E-mail: info@kevinmayhewltd.com

www.kevinmayhew.com

9 8 7 6 5 4 3 2 1 0

ISBN 978 1 84867 204 8
Catalogue No. 1501195

Cover design by Rob Mortonson
Edited by Alison Evans
Typeset by Richard Weaver

Printed and bound in Great Britain

Contents

About the author	6
Introduction	7
Advent 1 – People of faith	13
Advent 2 – People of vision	19
Advent 3 – People immersed in God	25
Advent 4 – People in love with God	31
Carol service	37
The Christmas story	43
The Epiphany	49
The Baptism of our Lord	55
Celebrating the water made wine	61
The mission of the Church	67
Candlemas – The presentation of Christ in the Temple	71

About the author

David Adam was the Vicar of Lindisfarne, off the Northumbrian coast, for thirteen years until he retired in March 2003. His work involved ministering to thousands of pilgrims and other visitors. He is the author of many inspiring books on spirituality and prayer, and his Celtic writings have rekindled a keen interest in our Christian heritage.

Introduction

The Advent, Christmas season is at the darkest time of the year and contains within it the shortest day. It is not surprising that this should be a time when we want to add light to our lives. Think about the saying: 'It is better to light a small candle than to complain about the darkness.' Every day in Advent I light a candle to affirm that Christ comes to conquer the darkness and that Christ is the Light of the World. Christmas and Advent are about the Light of Christ coming into our lives, coming to each of us, and to the world. Not only should we welcome and rejoice in this light, we should share it with others. The Advent to Candlemas season is when we celebrate the fact that 'the people who walked in darkness have seen a great light; those who lived in a land of deep darkness – on them the light has shined' (Isaiah 9:2).

All of the services in this book have built into them a candle lighting. This begins with only one candle on Advent Sunday and increases by a candle each of the four weeks of Advent until on Christmas day we light a fifth candle for Jesus the Light come into the world. For the forty days of the Christmas season we welcome the Light of Christ and his revealing to the world. The culmination of the forty days of Christmas is Candlemas where we take the light into our hands and hearts as we turn towards the next season of Lent to Easter.

Though you may not want to use the whole service at home, it is easy to extract the candle lighting and the intercessions and use them as part of your daily worship. The candle lighting is a good way to welcome the dawn of a new day and used as evening prayers a way of committing our lives to our God. Although it is assumed that as Advent progresses you will light more candles until five are lit each week, you may choose to light only one candle and say the prayers as you do that. However there is something special about the increasing of light to show in symbol the increasing of faith, of vision, of proclamation and the coming of Christ into the world.

The Advent candles are normally held together in an Advent wreath. To make an Advent wreath to hold the candles of Advent and Christmas is quite simple. First, from a florist, obtain a circle of Oasis and add to it greenery (this reminds us we are dealing with eternal events). Now add four candles; some people like to use purple candles to say it is Advent. In the centre of the circle add one larger white candle to represent Christ's arrival, God with us. Advent is at the darkest time of the year, so it is good to bring a little light to it. The first week we will light one candle, the second two, by Christmas we will light all five. Then we will continue to light the five each week until Candlemas. We will need to replace any burnt-out candles with new ones. The burnt-out candles are symbols of those who have given their life to Christ and in the renewing of them we should offer our life to God. To make a simpler wreath use tea-lights on a tea plate with four around the outside and one in the centre, again replace any that burn out. With the simple wreath you can add a little greenery if you so wish.

The structure of most of the services has four sections: the Affirmation of God's presence, the Candle lighting, the Ministry of the Word, and the Response ending with the Blessing. Into this structure there should be woven times of silence and stillness. I have suggested a time of stillness within each section.

Affirmation of God's presence

Affirmation
Invitation to worship
Hymn
Silence

Candle lighting

Silence

Ministry of the Word

Reading
Hymn
The Gospel
Sermon
Silence
Hymn

Response

Creed
Confession
Thanksgiving
Intercessions
Collect
The Lord's Prayer
Silence
Hymn

Blessing

The traditional prayers and creed are as used throughout the Christian Church, the Confession is taken from the Anglican book of Common Worship. Though I have suggested hymns, these are there only as guidelines. Many of the suggestions within the structure could be easily included within a Service of Morning or Evening Prayer, or Holy Communion. The important thing throughout is to let it be seen we are welcoming the coming of the Light of Christ into our lives and our world.

Traditional prayers

In the name of the Father and of the Son and of the Holy Spirit. Amen.

The Lord's Prayer

Our Father, who art in heaven,
hallowed be thy name;
thy kingdom come;
thy will be done;
on earth as it is in heaven.
Give us this day our daily bread.
And forgive us our trespasses,
as we forgive those who trespass against us.

And lead us not into temptation;
but deliver us from evil.
For thine is the kingdom,
the power and the glory,
for ever and ever. Amen.

The Kyrie

Lord, have mercy.
Lord, have mercy.

Christ, have mercy.
Christ, have mercy.

Lord, have mercy.
Lord, have mercy.

The Apostles' Creed

I believe in God, the Father almighty,
creator of heaven and earth,
and in Jesus Christ, his only Son our Lord,
who was conceived by the Holy Spirit,
born of the Virgin Mary,
suffered under Pontius Pilate,
was crucified, died and was buried;
he descended to the dead.
The third day he rose again;
he ascended into heaven,
he is seated at the right hand of the Father,
and will come to judge the living and the dead.

I believe in the Holy Spirit,
the holy catholic Church,
the communion of saints,
the forgiveness of sins,
the resurrection of the body,
and the life everlasting. Amen.

Confession

Most merciful God,
Father of our Lord Jesus Christ,
we confess that we have sinned
in thought, word and deed.
We have not loved you with our whole heart.
We have not loved our neighbours as ourselves.
In your mercy
forgive what we have been,
help us to amend what we are,
and direct what we shall be;
that we may do justly,
love mercy,
and walk humbly with you, our God. Amen.
(Common Worship – Daily Prayer p.96)

Absolution

Almighty God have mercy upon us,
forgive us our sins
and keep us in the fullness of life eternal,
through Jesus Christ our Lord. Amen.

Advent 1
People of faith

Affirmation of God's presence

Affirmation

Advent is a time when we rejoice in the coming of Christ into our lives, that he came at Christmas, and that he comes again to be our Lord and King.

Advent celebrates that our God comes to us again and again.

Today is the First Sunday in Advent when we remember our ancestors in the faith and give thanks to God for all of his faithful people.

Invitation to worship

With all the faithful we rejoice in the presence, in the peace and in the power of God, Father, Son and Holy Spirit. Amen.

The Lord is here.
His Spirit is with us.

Hymn

Hark the glad sound! the Saviour comes

Silence

Candle lighting

On the First Sunday in Advent we light one candle to say with all faithful people:

The Lord comes to us.
He abides with us.

When our lives are darkened it is necessary to celebrate the presence that comes to us and the light that is given to us.
(The lighting of the Advent candle)

Jesus Christ is the Light of the World:
eternal light shine in our hearts.

When this world is as dark as night,
you are the one we call the Light.
Come, Lord Jesus.

When we are tempted to go astray,
you are the one we call the Way.
Come, Lord Jesus.

When the storms of life increase,
you are the one we call our Peace.
Come, Lord Jesus.

When troubles to our lives bring harm,
you are the one who brings us calm.
Come, Lord Jesus.

Blessed are you Lord our God, for you have called us out of darkness into your glorious light. We thank you for all our ancestors in the faith, for Abraham and Sarah, Isaac and Rebekah, Jacob and Rachel, for all who have passed on the faith to us. You are their God and our God, their Father and our Father. Help us to know that as you came to them you come to us.
Blessed be God forever.

Silence

Ministry of the Word

Reading

Hebrews 11:6, 8–10, 23–27

Hymn

Lord of our life, and God of our salvation

The Gospel

Matthew 8:5–13

Sermon

Silence

Hymn

Have faith in God, my heart

Response

Creed

Confession

Thanksgiving

Praise and thanks to you, O God, for you have created us out of your love and for your love. You give us the opportunity to know you and to serve you. We give you thanks for all who have revealed your friendship in their lives. We thank you for our ancestors in the faith to whom you spoke as a friend. We rejoice that you have called us to be part of this household of faith, through Christ our Lord. Amen.

Intercessions

Blessed are you Lord our God for you are an ever-present help in our troubles, you are our strength and our salvation. We come before you in faith and seek your love.

We thank you for the Church throughout the world and for all who have kept faith in you. We ask your blessing upon all who are being persecuted for their faith, all who are being scorned or rejected because of their beliefs. We ask you to give new courage and hope to those who have lost faith and all who walk in darkness.
God of faith,
increase our love and trust in you.

We give thanks for the land in which we live and we ask your blessing upon all who are leaders in government and in society. May they be people of vision and committed to justice. We ask your blessing upon any who are suffering from disasters, from flood or famine and all who are uncertain of their future.
God of faith,
increase our love and trust in you.

We thank you for all the love we have received and we ask you to protect and guide all our friends and loved ones. Bless our homes and our families and enfold them in your love. We pray especially today for any who are suffering from the breakdown of family life or from broken relationships and all who have lost faith in others.
God of faith,
increase our love and trust in you.

We thank you for our well-being and we remember before you all who are ill or suffering, all who are finding life overwhelming and all who cannot cope. We pray especially for those who feel no one cares and are lonely.
God of faith,
increase our love and trust in you.

We join our prayers with all the faithful who have gone before and put our hope and trust in you.
Merciful Father,
accept these prayers for the sake of your Son, our Saviour Jesus Christ. Amen.

Collect

Almighty God, give us grace to cast away the works of darkness
and to put on the armour of light
now in the time of this mortal life,
in which your Son Jesus Christ came to visit us in great humility;
that on the last day
when he shall come again in his glorious majesty
to judge the living and the dead,

we may rise to the life immortal;
through him who is alive and reigns with you,
in the unity of the Holy Spirit,
one God, now and for ever.
Amen.

(Common Worship Collect for Advent 1)

The Lord's Prayer

Silence

Hymn

Thou didst leave thy throne

Blessing

God the Father give you grace to know him and to love him;
Christ the Son grant you an awareness of his saving power;
the Holy Spirit guide you in the way of faithfulness and truth;
and the blessing of God Almighty, the Father, the Son and the Holy Spirit
be upon you and your loved ones this day and for always. Amen.

Advent 2
People of vision

Affirmation of God's presence

Affirmation

Advent is a time when we rejoice in the coming of Christ into our lives, that he came at Christmas, and that he comes again to be our Lord and King.

Advent celebrates that our God comes to us again and again.

Today is the Second Sunday in Advent when we remember the prophets and give thanks for all people of vision.

Invitation to worship

With all the prophets and people of vision we rejoice in the grace and goodness of God, Father, Son and Holy Spirit. Amen.

The Lord is here.
His Spirit is with us.

Hymn

Be thou my vision, O Lord of my heart

Silence

Candle lighting

On the Second Sunday in Advent we light two candles, one for all of God's faithful people and one for men and women of vision.

When our lives are darkened it is necessary to celebrate the presence that comes to us and the vision that is given to us.

The Lord comes to us
He abides with us.
(The lighting of the two Advent candles)

Jesus Christ is the Light of the World:
eternal light, shine in our hearts.

Lord, open our eyes to your presence.
Come, Lord of light.

Lord, open our ears to your call.
Come, Lord of light.

Lord, open our hearts to your love.
Come, Lord of light.

Lord, open our lives to your guiding.
Come, Lord of light.

Blessed are you Lord God for you open the eyes of the blind. You gave vision and insight to the prophets. We thank you for Amos and Hosea, for Isaiah, Jeremiah and Ezekiel and all the prophets, and for all people who have extended our awareness through their vision. You are their God and our God, their Father and our Father. Help us to know that as you came to them you come to us.
Blessed be God forever.

Silence

Ministry of the Word

Reading

Isaiah 9:2, 3, 6, 7

Hymn

Come, thou long-expected Jesus

The Gospel

Luke 10:23, 24

Sermon

Silence

Hymn

Long ago the prophets knew

Response

Creed

Confession

Thanksgiving

Praise and thanks to you, Lord our God, for you give us sight and insight, eyes to see you and hearts to love you. We thank you for the beauty of the world and the glory of creation. We praise you for the many colours of nature and for the brightness of the sun. We thank you for all who have looked deeply and been aware of you and your working: we thank you for the prophets and all people of vision. Amen.

Intercessions

Good and gracious God, open our eyes to your presence and our hearts to your love.
Bless all who seek to know you and proclaim you.
We remember all who study the scriptures and all who seek to be still before you.
Lord, guide all who would lead us to a deep awareness of you.
We ask your blessing upon all ministers and preachers and all who teach religious studies.
Lord, open our eyes to your presence
and our hearts to your love.

Lord, direct all who seek to influence our lives and our thoughts through their own vision.
Bless all who are doing research and all who are seeking to conserve what is good.

We remember before you all politicians, scientists, musicians, artists and craftspeople, and all who through their vision are enriching our lives.
Lord, open our eyes to your presence
and our hearts to your love.

Strengthen and bless all who are striving to enhance and uphold family life. Help us to see where we can increase our love and care. We remember before you all who feel neglected or lonely. May we prove to be good neighbours where we can.
Lord, open our eyes to your presence
and our hearts to your love.

We give thanks for all who have used their insight for healing and medical research. We ask your blessing upon all doctors, nurses and all involved in healing and wholeness. We bring before you friends and loved ones who are ill or struggling at this time.
Lord, open our eyes to your presence
and our hearts to your love.

Lord, extend our vision that we may know your presence and see our life as in your hands. Bless all our loved ones who are departed from us and grant that they may enjoy the vision of your glory.
Merciful Father,
accept these prayers for the sake of your Son, our Saviour Jesus Christ. Amen.

Collect

God be in my head, and in my understanding.
God be in my eyes, and in my looking.
God be in my mouth, and in my speaking.
God be in my heart, and in my thinking.
God be at my end, and at my departing.
Amen.

(Sarum Book of Hours 1514)

The Lord's Prayer

Silence

Hymn

God has spoken – by the prophets

Blessing

The Lord grant you a vision of his presence,
an awareness of his love,
a sensitivity to his guiding,
and the blessing of God Almighty, the Father, the Son and the Holy Spirit
be upon you and your loved ones this day and for always. Amen.

Advent 3
People immersed in God

Affirmation of God's presence

Affirmation

Advent is a time when we rejoice in the coming of Christ into our lives, that he came at Christmas, and that he comes again to be our Lord and King.

Advent celebrates that our God comes to us again and again.

Today is the Third Sunday in Advent, a day when we remember John the Baptist and all who turn towards God to serve him.

Invitation to worship

With John the Baptist and all God's faithful we immerse ourselves in the love, light and leading of God, Father, Son and Holy Spirit. Amen.

The Lord is here.
His Spirit is with us.

Hymn

Hark! a thrilling voice is sounding

Silence

Candle lighting

On the Third Sunday in Advent we light three candles, one for all of God's faithful people, one for men and women of vision, and one for John the Baptist and all who immerse themselves in the love and presence of God.

When our lives are darkened it is necessary to celebrate the presence that comes to us and the light that is given to us.
The Lord comes to us.
He abides with us.
(The lighting of the three Advent candles)

Jesus Christ is the Light of the World:
eternal light shine in our hearts.

Father you created us by your love and for your love.
May we abide in you and you in us.

Jesus you redeemed us by your love and for your love.
May we abide in you and you in us.

Spirit of God you guide us by your love and for your love.
May we abide in you and you in us.

Holy and Blessed Three your love enfolds and surrounds us.
May we abide in you and you in us.

Blessed are you, Lord our God, for you sent your messenger John the Baptist to prepare the way and make ready for your coming, that we may be prepared and ready to receive and welcome you into our lives and homes. As you come to us in love may we abide in your love and in your presence this day and for ever. Blessed be God, Father, Son and Holy Spirit.
Blessed be God forever.

Silence

Ministry of the Word

Reading

Isaiah 40:1–11

Hymn

On Jordan's bank the Baptist's cry

The Gospel

Matthew 3:1–12

Sermon

Silence

Hymn

The advent of our King

Response

Creed

Confession

Thanksgiving

O God, we give you thanks and praise for all who have prepared the way for us to know you and to love you. We thank you for John the Baptist, that he prepared the people for the coming of Jesus. We remember in thanksgiving those who have taught us the faith by word and by example and all who have led us to you by art, music and writings. We give thanks for our baptism and the knowledge that we dwell in you and you in us. To you, O Lord our God, be praise and glory now and forever.

Intercessions

Holy and Mighty God, as we give thanks for John the Baptist, we ask your blessing upon all who prepare the way for others to know you and to love you. Guide with your wisdom all who prepare people for baptism or confirmation. We remember all who lead worship or study groups and all who speak of your presence and your power.
Lord, may we witness
that we dwell in you and you in us.

Holy and Mighty God we give thanks for all who prepare young people to live their lives fully. We ask your blessing upon all who are involved in education, and all who influence our minds through the press, the media and their words and their actions. Guide with your wisdom all that are called to govern and to make decisions about the

future of our world. Lord may we all be prepared to live simply that others might simply live. May we all work for justice, righteous dealing and for freedom.
Lord, may we witness
that we dwell in you and you in us.

Holy and Mighty God we ask your blessing upon our homes and our loved ones. We remember all who are preparing for the Christmas season and pray that they may make in their lives a place for you. We remember all who will feel lonely or neglected at this season.
Lord, may we witness
that we dwell in you and you in us.

Holy and Mighty God we give thanks for the grace of forgiveness and the opportunity to turn to you and your love. We ask your blessing upon all who are consumed with guilt or who cannot allow forgiveness for themselves or others. We remember all who are in prison and those who are suffering for their faith and their witness to you.
Lord, may we witness
that we dwell in you and you in us.

Holy and Mighty God we remember before you all who are terminally ill and are being prepared for death. May they find in you courage and hope through the promise of life eternal.
Merciful Father,
accept these prayers for the sake of your Son, Jesus Christ our Lord. Amen.

Collect

O Lord Jesus Christ,
who at your first coming sent your messenger
to prepare your way before you:
grant that the ministers and stewards of your mysteries
may likewise so prepare and make ready your way
by turning the hearts of the disobedient
to the wisdom of the just,
that at your second coming to judge the world

we may be found an acceptable people in your sight;
for you are alive and reign with the Father
in the unity of the Holy Spirit,
one God, now and forever. Amen.

(Common Worship Collect for Advent 3)

The Lord's Prayer

Silence

Hymn

We are marching in the light of God

Blessing

The love of the Father strengthen you,
the love of Jesus surround you,
the love of the Spirit guide you,
and the blessing of God Almighty, the Father, the Son and the Holy Spirit
be upon you and your loved ones this day and for always. Amen.

Advent 4
People in love with God

Affirmation of God's presence

Affirmation

Advent is a time when we rejoice in the coming of Christ into our lives, that he came at Christmas, and that he comes again to be our Lord and King.

Advent celebrates that our God comes to us again and again.

Today is the Fourth Sunday in Advent when we remember the Blessed Virgin Mary and give thanks for all who love God and seek to do his will.

Invitation to worship

With the Blessed Virgin Mary we rejoice in the God who comes to us. We are in power and presence of God, Father, Son and Holy Spirit. Amen.

The Lord is here.
His Spirit is with us.

Hymn

Love divine, all loves excelling

Silence

Candle lighting

On the Fourth Sunday in Advent we light four candles, one for all of God's faithful people, one for men and women of vision, and one for John the Baptist and all who immerse themselves in the love and presence of God. The fourth candle is for the Blessed Virgin Mary and all who give themselves to God in love.

When our lives are darkened it is necessary to celebrate the presence that comes to us and the light that is given to us.
The Lord comes to us.
He abides with us.
(The lighting of the four Advent candles)

Jesus Christ is the Light of the World:
eternal light shine in our hearts.

In Christ Jesus the darkness is defeated:
the light has come into the world. *(Light candle one)*
Emmanuel, God is with us.

In Christ Jesus a new day has dawned:
the light has come into the world. *(Light candle two)*
Emmanuel, God is with us.

In Christ Jesus is our hope and joy:
the light has come into the world. *(Light candle three)*
Emmanuel, God is with us.

In Christ Jesus life is eternal:
the light has come into the world. *(Light candle four)*
Emmanuel, God is with us.

Blessed are you Lord our God, for in the fullness of time you shared in our humanity being born of the Blessed Virgin Mary. You came down to lift us up: you became human that we might share in the divine. As we rejoice in Mary doing your will and so welcoming you into her life may we abide in you and know that you abide in us. Blessed are you Father, Son and Holy Spirit.
Blessed be God for ever.

Silence

Ministry of the Word

Reading

Isaiah 7:10 –15

Hymn

Tell out, my soul

The Gospel

Luke 1:26–38

Sermon

Silence

Hymn

O come, O come, Emmanuel

Response

Creed

Confession

Thanksgiving

Lord God we give you thanks and praise for the angel Gabriel and the message he brought to Mary. We thank you for her acceptance, her obedience and her joy. We rejoice that through Mary our Saviour came to dwell among us.

May we learn the obedience of Mary, serving you with joy and accepting Jesus into our lives. We rejoice that you are her God and our God: you are her Father and our Father. Help us to know that as you came to Mary you come to us and through us your will can be done.

Intercessions

O God, as we celebrate your coming among us, we seek to give our love to you. In our daily living let us seek to do your will and help to bring in your kingdom.

Through all who seek to obey to you,
through all who quietly witness to your presence,
through our faithfulness in prayer,

through our working for your glory,
through all reaching out in mission,
in our love and obedience,
your kingdom come.

Through all who desire righteousness and freedom,
through all who strive for peace,
through all that are caring for the poor,
through those who seek to improve your world,
in our love and obedience,
your kingdom come.

Through all our relationships,
through our love in our homes,
through our community and our society,
through our daily work and our talents,
in our love and obedience,
your kingdom come.

Through those who provide places of healing and shelter,
through the caring professions,
through all who look after the ill and lonely,
through all who show compassion and care,
in our love and obedience,
your kingdom come.

We remember especially today the love and obedience of Mary and ask your prayers for all faithful people. We remember loved ones and friends who are now departed from us; may they rejoice in your eternal kingdom.
Merciful Father,
accept these prayers for the sake of your Son, Jesus Christ our Lord. Amen.

Collect

God our redeemer,
who prepared the Blessed Virgin Mary
to be the mother of your Son:

grant that, as she looked for his coming as our Saviour,
so we may be ready to greet him
when he comes again as our judge;
who is alive and reigns with you,
in the unity of the Holy Spirit,
one God, now and forever.
Amen.

(Common Worship Collect for Advent 4)

The Lord's Prayer

Silence

Hymn

It is a thing most wonderful

Blessing

God give you grace to follow the example of Mary and to welcome the Christ into your lives and homes.
The Holy Spirit overshadow you and protect you,
and the blessing of God Almighty, the Father, the Son and the Holy Spirit be upon you and your loved ones this day and for always. Amen.

Carol service

Material needed: Advent wreath, or five candles plus one more candle; crib figures including an angel, wise men optional. Candles with drip shields for everyone optional.

Carol

Once in royal David's city

This holy night (day), we give thanks for the coming of the Lord of Glory. Jesus not only comes to Bethlehem, he comes to us, today. He comes to our world, our homes, and our loved ones. Let us make room for him and rejoice at his coming. Come and share in the love of Mary and Joseph: join in the song of the angels and share in the wonder of the shepherds. Above all let us give ourselves to him, for he gives himself to us.

The hope of glory

Reading

Isaiah 9:2, 6, 7

Prayer

Father, on this holy night (day) our Saviour came as light into our darkness and revealed his love for the whole world. Open our eyes to his presence and our hearts to his love that we may know him as the Prince of Peace and Lord of Light.

The lighting of the four Advent candles

Have four people, with lighted tapers, come from different corners of the church. (This can be more effective if the lights are left off until the Advent candles are lit, or off all the time if it is a service by candlelight.)

Let the first person begin by saying, 'Emmanuel' and asking the congregation to say, '**The Lord is with us. Amen**' every time it is said and to say it loudly. In turn let the people with tapers come down the church and light a single candle. After each one lights a candle they say 'Emmanuel' and the congregation respond.

As the four people light the candles, each has a sentence to say:

The Christ is come into the world.
Emmanuel,
the Lord is with us. Amen.

Jesus is born among us.
Emmanuel,
the Lord is with us. Amen.

Our God has taken upon him our flesh.
Emmanuel,
the Lord is with us. Amen.

This is the light that defeats the darkness.
Emmanuel,
the Lord is with us. Amen.

Prayer

Blessed are you Lord our God for in your deep love for us you have shared in our humanity that we might share in your glory. Help us to make room in our lives to be aware of you and of your coming to us through Jesus Christ the Word made flesh. Amen.

Carol

Of the Father's love begotten

Glory in the darkness

Reading

John 1:1–5

The lighting of the Christ candle

This night (day) the Saviour promised long is come.
Emmanuel,
the Lord is with us. Amen.

The Saviour comes among us and is here.
Emmanuel,
the Lord is with us. Amen.

His light shines in darkness that is about us. *(Light the candle)*
Emmanuel,
the Lord is with us. Amen.

Prayer

Father on this holy night (day) made resplendent with the glory of the true Light, grant that we who have known the mystery of that Light on earth, may enter into the fullness of his joys in heaven. Amen.

(Ancient Western Rite, adapted)

If the service is to be by candlelight then let everyone have their candles lit from the Christ candle or from a person who has passed on this light.

Carol

Silent night

The promise of glory

Reading

Luke 1:26–38

Prayer

Father on this holy night (day) your promise to Mary is fulfilled. Jesus Christ our Saviour comes down and takes upon him our flesh. As he shares in our humanity may we share in his divinity through him who is Christ the Lord.

Carol

O little town of Bethlehem
(During the carol Joseph and Mary are placed in the stable)

Glory in the night

Reading

Luke 2:1–7

Prayer

Father on this holy night (day) Joseph and Mary could find no room at the inn and the Christ was born in the stable. We remember before you all who are homeless, all poor people and refugees.
Lord, hear us.
Lord, mercifully hear us.

Carol

Away in a manger
(Jesus is brought and placed in the stable)

Angels of glory

Reading

Luke 2:8–14

Prayer

Father on this holy night (day) the holy angels sang 'Peace on earth and good will to all'. Grant us your peace, Lord, in our hearts and in our homes: peace in all our dealings and peace in our world.
Lord, hear us.
Lord, mercifully hear us.

Carol

Hark, the herald-angels sing
(The Angel is placed above the stable. If the crib set does not have an angel cut some from old Christmas cards and at this point have them placed above the crib. Though there are many beautiful Christmas angels that could be bought to add to your crib.)

Glory come to earth

Reading

Luke 2:15–20

Prayer

Father on this holy night (day) the shepherds heard the songs of angels. They travelled to Bethlehem to see Jesus and they gave to you praise and glory for all they had seen and heard. Make us aware of the presence of our Lord that we also may give you praise and glory. We remember all whose lives are shrouded with darkness and who need the light of Christ.
Lord, hear us.
Lord, mercifully hear us.

Carol

While shepherds watched
(The shepherds (and sheep) are placed in the stable)

Glory for everyone

Reading

Matthew 2:1–12

Prayer

Father on this holy night (day) your love was revealed for all people in all places. We ask your blessing upon all pilgrim people and all who are seekers.
Lord, hear us.
Lord, mercifully hear us.

Carol

We three kings of Orient are
(The kings can be placed on window sills around the church or at various points as they are still meant to be travelling. A lit candle is placed near the stable to represent us, because we love Jesus and we know he loves us.)

We have seen his glory

Reading

John 10–14

Blessed are you, Lord our God, for you have revealed your glory and your love in the face of our Lord Jesus Christ: for us and for our salvation he has come to dwell among us. He has shared in our humanity that we might share in his divinity. Blessed are you Father, Son and Holy Spirit.

As our Saviour has taught us, so we pray:
(The Lord's Prayer)

The blessing of the crib

God our Father, we thank you for Jesus born of the Blessed Virgin Mary and that he came to live among us. As we rejoice in his birth, we ask you to bless this crib that all who see it may be reminded of your love and your presence with us. May it help to bring his light into the darkness of our world: through the same Christ who abides with us and reigns with you and the Holy Spirit, one God now and forever. Amen.

Carol

O come, all ye faithful

Blessing

Give glory to God who loves us with an everlasting love.
The presence of the Mighty God be with you,
the love of the Everlasting Father enfold you,
the peace of the Prince of Peace surround you,
the light of the Wonderful Counsellor guide you,
and the blessing of God Almighty, the Father, the Son and the
Holy Spirit, be upon you and your homes and loved ones now and
for evermore. Amen.

The Christmas story

Materials needed: a set of crib figures, including an angel, and two candles. Let the teller of the story sit as close to the children as possible for the readings. I usually place my script inside a large Christmas card.

Welcome

Welcome to you all who have come to give thanks to God for his love and for Jesus being born into the world. We will begin by being very quiet.

We are in the presence and in the love of God, Father, Son and Holy Spirit.
The Lord is with you.
And also with you.

Lord Jesus, help us to love you like Mary and Joseph,
to worship with the angels,
to come to you with the shepherds,
to give our lives to you like the wise men.
Help us to celebrate your birthday with joy.

There was no room for you at the inn –
let us make room in our hearts for you.
You were born in a stable –
we pray for all without a home or people to love them.
Mary and Joseph gave you a home – bless our homes today.
The angels sang your praises – may we sing to you with joy.
The shepherds came to see you – may we seek to know you.
You came because you love us – help us to love you.

Christ, our Lord, come to earth,
bless our homes by your birth.
Christ born in a manger stall,
bless our loved ones one and all.

Christ a baby, yet God and King,
bless us now as to you we sing.

Carol

O little town of Bethlehem

The Christmas story

Once a very long time ago there was a little town called 'The House of Bread' – we call it Bethlehem. There in the quiet of the night the wonderful Christmas story happened.

Now in the village of Bethlehem there was an inn, a place where people could come and stay. We do not know its name but let us pretend we can hear its sign creaking as it swings in the wind. The innkeeper should have put some oil on it but he has been too busy for the inn is full of people. It would be hard to make room for any more. This is because the government has made a law that everyone must go to the place where they were born and there have their name written down in a big book. There were lots and lots of people on all of the roads. The inn was already packed full. Inside there was singing and dancing. People were meeting family and friends and telling stories. It was all very busy and noisy.

But outside it was still and quiet. Out of the back door, past the well where they got water, past the sleeping hens, the goats and the sheep there was a stable, a cattle shed. It was quiet there except for the sound of the cow and the donkey breathing. Imagine their warm breath coming out of their mouths, for it was a cold night. From the stable you can see the stars shining. One very bright star seems to be shining right on to the stable. While we sing our carol the cow and the donkey will go to the stable.

Carol

Little donkey

So there in the quiet the animals rest and wait, breathing quietly in the cold night air. A bright star shines upon them.

Let us go again to the front of the inn. We stand under the sign and look down the road. The road shines in the moonlight. Two people are coming down the road very slowly. They look like shadows in the distance. As they come nearer we see they are a man and a young woman. They have come a long way and the woman is very tired. They can only move slowly for the woman is going to have a baby.

We know what no one in Bethlehem knows, the baby will be born tonight. The man is Joseph the Carpenter, who makes things with wood. The lady is Mary and soon she is to be the mother of the baby Jesus.

They look at the creaking sign and then they knock hard on the door. For a while no one comes. At last the innkeeper comes wiping his hands. He has too many people to look after. There is no room for any more. He is sorry but he cannot help. Almost as he closed the door he stopped. Mary and Joseph looked so tired, he was sorry for them. He said, 'You can sleep in the stable if you want to. You will have to share it with the animals.' Mary and Joseph were so relieved. The innkeeper showed them around the side of the inn. As they passed the well they could hear the singing and dancing of the crowds. They went past the sheep and the goats into the quiet stable. It looked as if it had been waiting for them. Mary thought this would be a better place than a crowded inn for her baby to be born. The cow and the donkey looked up as if to welcome them. The innkeeper gave them a lantern light and left them to settle down for the night. While we sing our next carol Mary and Joseph will be taken and placed in the stable.

Carol

Silent night

The cow and the donkey, Mary and Joseph are settled in the stable. There by the light of the lantern we watch big shadows dancing on the walls. It looks as if darkness and light are having a fight. Suddenly a baby cries – for Jesus is born. God who loves us and all the world has sent his Son into the world. Jesus is born of Mary. As his mother, Mary will look after him. With Joseph's help Jesus is washed. Then his little body is rubbed gently with salt! That is to be like a medicine to stop Jesus being poorly. Then Jesus is carefully wrapped up in bands of cloth to keep him safe and warm. He is sleepy so Joseph puts him in the manger of hay to sleep.

Look, here is the baby Jesus for the crib. See how tiny he looks in this church, but not as tiny as Jesus looked in the great big dark world. While we sing our next carol the baby Jesus will be carefully carried and put in the stable. We will also light a candle . . . It goes to stand beside the stable to show that a special light has come into the world. This light tells us of the love of God. This is the light of Jesus Christ.

Carol

Away in a manger

Now away from the inn and high up on the hillsides it was dark and cold. There in the night men were working. They were shepherds and they were looking after their sheep in the dark. They were very brave for they were guarding their sheep against wolves or robbers. They were keeping watch, looking out on the night. Some were sitting close to a fire to keep warm. It was a cold night and the stars shone like jewels in the sky. Isaac, that is the name of one of the shepherds, threw a large piece of wood onto the fire. It caused sparks to fly upwards, they rose higher and higher as if they were trying to reach the stars. Suddenly the light grew brighter, it was as if the sparks were taking on a shape, and there was something strange in the sky. The light got brighter and it was coming nearer and nearer. Isaac wondered if he was dreaming – now he was afraid. What was it? Then there was the most beautiful singing that he had ever heard. Voices from out of this world, for angels were singing a lovely song. The shepherds were very still and listened to the words, 'Glory to God in the highest and on earth peace. Glory to God in the highest and on earth peace.'

Look, here is our angel. Let us all be still and quiet while it is taken to be near the stable.

Carol

The Virgin Mary had a baby boy

The brave shepherds were afraid. But an angel said, 'Do not be afraid for I bring you good news – good tidings of great joy. This will make you happy. Today, this very night, in Bethlehem, the city of David, a Saviour is born. It is Christ the Lord. God has sent him because he loves you and all people. Go to Bethlehem and this is what you will find: a baby wrapped up in bands of cloth and lying in a manger. The angel stopped speaking and again the shepherds heard the angels' song, 'Glory to God in the highest and on earth peace.' Then it was suddenly very quiet because the angels had gone. The night was dark again and the shepherds were all alone on the hillside. They rubbed their eyes and looked at the sky and then at each other. They wondered if they had dreamt it but it was real.

'Come,' said one of them, 'let us go to Bethlehem and see this wonderful baby.' So taking their shepherd's crooks and their youngest sheepdog they set off. The older dogs were left to protect the sheep. By now Bethlehem was very quiet; everyone was sleeping, or trying to, except for Mary and Joseph who were looking after the baby.

During the singing of our next carol the shepherds will make their way to the stable to see Jesus.

Carol

While shepherds watched

The shepherds tiptoed across the rustling straw and bowed down to look at the little baby. They all stood very quiet and still just looking at Jesus. They were all giving their love to the baby. Mary his mother, Joseph who would look after Mary and the baby, and the shepherds; all of them worshipping Jesus. This is what we are called to do, to be quiet before Jesus and to give our love to him. We are to make our church like the stable at Bethlehem and worship the new born King. It is here that Jesus comes to us, he wants to give his love to us and for us to give our love to him. Let us close our eyes, and hear again the song of the angels, 'Glory to God in the highest and on earth peace.' They say to us, 'To you is born this day in the city of David, in Bethlehem, a Saviour who is Christ the Lord.' Let us be still and quiet and say thank you to God for Jesus and to Jesus for coming to live on earth.

While we sing someone will light a candle from the Jesus candle and put it near the crib. This candle is for us because we love Jesus and we know he loves us.

Now let us sing:

O come, let us adore him,
O come, let us adore him,
O come, let us adore him,
Christ the Lord.

The blessing of the crib

Praise and thanks to you, Lord our God, for you have sent your Son, Jesus, to come into the world. We thank you for Mary and Joseph and their love for Jesus. We thank you for the angels and for the shepherds and for all who welcomed Jesus into the world. May we also give our love to him this day and always.

As Jesus our Saviour has taught us, so we pray:
(The Lord's Prayer)

God our Father, we thank you for Jesus born of the Blessed Virgin Mary and that he came to live among us. As we rejoice in his birth, we ask you to bless this crib that all who see it may be reminded of your love and your presence with us. May it help to bring his light into the darkness of our world: through the same Christ who abides with us and reigns with you and the Holy Spirit, one God now and forever. Amen.

Carol

O come, all ye faithful

Blessing

God go with you and be known in your homes;
let Christ our Lord be known to live among you;
the Holy Spirit of God go with you and guide you
and the blessing of God Almighty, the Father, the Son and the Holy Spirit
be upon you and your loved ones this day and for always. Amen.

The Epiphany

Affirmation of God's presence

Affirmation

We celebrate today that Jesus is revealed to the wise men, who were not Jews, and so we rejoice in Jesus being revealed to all peoples.

Invitation to worship

God reveals himself to us. We are in the light and love of the Lord, Father, Son and Holy Spirit.
The Lord is here.
His Spirit is with us.

May Christ the daystar dawn in our hearts
and triumph over the shades of night.
(Common Worship, Daily Prayer p.108)

Hymn

O worship the Lord in the beauty of holiness
(If possible have a star on a pole to lead the procession into church. Let children carry in the figures of the three wise men. Have three children dressed as wise men with their gifts and five other children to carry the Advent and Christmas candles. They will all go to their seats or stand in silence until the candle lighting.)

Silence

Candle lighting

The people who walked in darkness have seen a great light. They lived in a land of shadows, but now light is shining upon them. You have given them great joy, O Lord; you have made them happy.

(Isaiah 9:2, 3)

Have five people light the candles, speaking the sentences as they do so.

Jesus, Word made flesh dwelling among us,
come, lighten our darkness. *(First candle is lit)*

Jesus born of the Blessed Virgin Mary,
come, lighten our darkness. *(Second candle is lit)*

Jesus adored by the wise men,
come, lighten our darkness. *(Third candle is lit)*

Jesus revealed to the world,
come, lighten our darkness. *(Fourth candle is lit)*

Jesus here and with us now,
come, lighten our darkness. *(Central candle is lit)*

The Word was made flesh and dwelt among us and we beheld his glory, as the glory of the only son of the Father full of grace and truth.

(John 1:14)

Blessed are you Lord our God for you have called us out of darkness to be children of light. The bright light of your presence scatters the darkness within us and is a lantern to our paths. Bless these lights that they may remind us of the light of your presence among us and your love for us all: through him who is the Light of the World, Jesus Christ our Lord. Amen.

Silence

Ministry of the Word

Reading

Isaiah 60:1–6, 19

Hymn

Earth has many a noble city

The Gospel

Matthew 2:1–12

Hymn

We three kings of Orient are

(During the chorus after verse one the star will be placed behind the crib)

Sermon

Prayer

O God, who brought wise men to Jesus by the guiding of a star, bring us to know and to love your Son, Jesus Christ our Lord. **Amen.**

We remember before you, O God, all who seek your presence, all who search for the truth, all who look for meaning and who desire to know you.
We ask your blessing upon all who are growing in faith and love.
Guide and go with all pilgrim peoples, especially those on their way to Bethlehem or Jerusalem.
Guide us, O Lord, in all our journeys throughout this life.
We pray for those who are new to our church or community.
Light of Christ,
shine in our lives.

(During verse two have the gold-bearing figure placed at the crib and the child dressed as the gold bearer should come to the crib)

Prayer

God, giver of all good gifts, as we remember the wise man bringing gold, we thank you for all that you have given to us and for your generous love.
We pray for the rich and the comfortable, all who have plenty of this world's goods: may they know that all things come from you and their lives are a gift from you. May the riches they have be put to good use for the benefit of the world.
We remember before you all who suffer from poverty, the world poor, the homeless and the hungry.
We ask your blessing upon all who feel their talents and gifts are not being used.
Light of Christ,
shine in our lives.

(During verse three have the incense-bearing figure placed at the crib and the child dressed as the incense bearer should come to the crib)

Prayer

God, Holy and Almighty One, as we remember the wise man bringing incense, we come to love and adore you. Bless us in our worship and help us to know your abiding presence and love.
We give thanks for all who come to you in worship and in wonder, all that are aware of awe or mystery in their lives.
We ask your blessing upon all leaders of worship, choirs and organists, upon all who give us a sense of wonder and beauty.
Light of Christ,
shine in our lives.

(During verse four have the myrrh-bearing figure placed at the crib and the child dressed as the myrrh bearer should come to the crib)

Prayer

God, as we remember the wise man bringing myrrh, we rejoice that you sent your Son into the world for us and for our salvation. He is our Healer and our Saviour.
We remember that he suffered and died for us and for our redemption.
We come with all who are in pain or sorrow, we remember those whose sickness finds no cure, the permanently ill and those with a short time to live.
We ask your blessing upon all doctors and nurses and any who are involved in relieving pain and in healing.
Light of Christ,
shine in our lives.

(At verse five the children dressed as wise men should kneel before the Christ child at the crib. During the final chorus let the children stand up and bow toward the Christ child and then go dancing back to their places.)

Prayer

Lord we worship and adore you.
We offer you our joys and sorrows, our sickness and health, our riches and our poverty.

We remember all who have enriched our lives by their goodness.
We ask your blessing upon our homes and loved ones.
We pray for loved ones who are now departed from us and are in the fullness of your kingdom.
Merciful Father,
accept these prayers for the sake of your Son, our Saviour Jesus Christ. Amen.

O God, who by the leading of a star brought the wise men to Bethlehem,
guide us through each day and night on our journey of faith.
Lord, give us the courage to persevere that we are not put off in our search for you.
May we witness to your gospel and rejoice in your glory.
May we seek to do your will until we enter the fullness of your kingdom.
We ask this in the name of him who came and lived among us, Jesus Christ our Lord.
Amen.

Silence

Hymn

As with gladness men of old

Response

Creed

Confession

Collect

O God, who by the leading of a star
manifested your only Son to the peoples of the earth:
mercifully grant that we,
who know you now by faith,
may behold your glory face to face;
through Jesus Christ our Lord.
Amen.

(Common Worship Collect for Epiphany)

The Lord's Prayer

Silence

Hymn

Christ is the world's true light

Blessing

Let the bright light of Christ enlighten your heart, shine in your life and direct your journeying.
Rejoice, for the light of Christ disperses the darkness of this world, and the blessing of God Almighty, the Father, the Son and the Holy Spirit be upon you and your loved ones now and always. Amen.

The Baptism of our Lord

Affirmation of God's presence

Affirmation

We come to give thanks for the Baptism of Jesus by John in the River Jordan. We rejoice that God's voice was heard affirming his Son and that the Holy Spirit was known to descend upon Jesus.

Invitation to worship

We are always immersed in the presence of God, Father, Son and Holy Spirit. Let us abide in him as he abides in us.
The Lord is here.
His Spirit is with us.

Hymn

Thou whose almighty word

Silence

Candle lighting

Today have the candle lighting near the font which is filled with water.

Have four people, with lighted tapers, in different corners of the church. Let a fifth person with a lighted taper stand in the centre of the church. (This can be more effective if the lights are left off until the candles are lit.)

Let one person begin by saying, 'We rejoice in the presence,' and asking the congregation to respond, '**of Father, Son and Holy Spirit**'. In turn let the people with tapers light a single candle. After each one lights a candle they say, 'We rejoice in the presence' and the congregation responds, '**of Father, Son and Holy Spirit.**'

1. I light this candle in thanksgiving for God the Father, the creator of light.
   We rejoice in the presence
   of Father, Son and Holy Spirit.

2. I light this candle in thanksgiving for Jesus Christ the Light of the World.
We rejoice in the presence
of Father, Son and Holy Spirit.

3. I light this candle in thanksgiving for the Holy Spirit who enlightens us all.
We rejoice in the presence
of Father, Son and Holy Spirit.

4. I light this candle in thanksgiving for the glory of the Holy Trinity.
We rejoice in the presence
of Father, Son and Holy Spirit.

5. I light this candle in thanksgiving for Jesus baptised for us and our salvation.
We rejoice in the presence
of Father, Son and Holy Spirit.

This is a good day to use the 'Peruvian Gloria' after the candle lighting or after the renewal of the baptismal vows.

After the Gospel reading the congregation can then renew their baptismal vows and have the opportunity to dip their finger in the water and sign themselves with the sign of the cross.

Silence

Ministry of the Word

Reading

Isaiah 65:17–25

Hymn

Spirit of God unseen as the wind

The Gospel

John 3:1–12

Sermon

Silence

Hymn

Christ, when for us you were baptised

Response

Renewal of baptismal vows

The Decision

In baptism, God calls us out of darkness into his marvellous light.
To follow Christ means dying to sin and rising to new life with him.
Therefore I ask:

Do you reject the devil and all rebellion against God?
I reject them.

Do you renounce the deceit and corruption of evil?
I renounce them.

Do you repent of the sins that separate us from God and neighbour?
I repent of them.

Do you turn to Christ as Saviour?
I turn to Christ.

Do you submit to Christ as Lord?
I submit to Christ.

Do you come to Christ, the way, the truth and the life?
I come to Christ.
(Common Worship, Services and Prayers for the Church of England p.143)

At this point the congregation can be invited to come to the font, dip their finger in the water and make the sign of the cross on their forehead. They can say:
I am signed with the cross for I belong to Christ.

Creed

Do you believe and trust in God the Father,
source of all being and life, the one for whom we exist?
I believe and trust in him.

Do you believe and trust in God the Son,
who took our human nature,
died for us and rose again?
I believe and trust in him.

Do you believe and trust in God the Holy Spirit,
who gives life to the people of God
and makes Christ known in the world?
I believe and trust in him.

This is the faith of the Church.
This is our faith.
We believe and trust in one God,
Father, Son and Holy Spirit.
(Common Worship, Services and Prayers for the Church of England p.143)

Confession

Thanksgiving

Praise and thanks to you Lord our God
for you have created all things from the beginning.
Praise and thanks to you Lord Jesus Christ;
you lived among us and were baptised of John.
Blessed are you Holy Spirit of power and might,
you descend as the dove filling us with life.
Blessed are you holy and blessed Three,
in you we live and move and have our being.
Amen.

Intercessions

Holy God, holy and strong One, holy and Mighty One,
thank you for our baptism and that you enfold us in love:
may we know that we dwell in you and you are in us.

Bless, O Lord, all who are baptised, may they rejoice in your abiding love.
We remember before you our godchildren and our godparents and all who have been baptised in this place, all who are being prepared for baptism or confirmation at this time.
Give to them and all your Church the power to show that we are members of Christ, children of God and inheritors of the kingdom of heaven.
Lord, we believe in you:
we trust in you.

Lord of all power and might, let your peace be known among us.
We remember all involved in conflict, those not at peace with themselves or with others.
Lord, bless all who are suffering from captivity or tyranny.
We remember for all who are slaves to debt or caught up in poverty.
Lord, we believe in you:
we trust in you.

We ask your blessing upon those who have shared their lives and their faith with us and upon all who have been concerned with our well-being.
Protect and bless our families and our friends, our neighbourhood and our land and keep us in your peace.
Lord, we believe in you:
we trust in you.

Bless all who are feeling lonely or anxious, those who are ill, those who have been involved in an accident or suffered from violence.
Give courage and hope to all who have suffered spiritually, physically or mentally, and to those with memories that disturb or frighten them.
Mighty God, comfort those who have lost confidence in themselves or in others.
We remember the world-weary, weak, and the sad.
Lord, we believe in you:
we trust in you.

We ask your blessing upon all your faithful people; we remember especially loved ones who are departed from us.
May they rejoice in that greater awareness of Father, Son and Holy Spirit and may we rejoice with them as inheritors of the kingdom of heaven.
Merciful Father,
accept these prayers for the sake of your Son, our Saviour Jesus Christ.
Amen.

Collect

Eternal Father,
who at the baptism of Jesus
revealed him to be your Son,
anointing him with the Holy Spirit:
grant to us, who are born again by water and the Spirit,
that we may be faithful to our calling as your adopted children;
through Jesus Christ our Lord.

(Common Worship Collect for The Baptism of Christ)

The Lord's Prayer

Silence

Hymn

Spirit of the living God, fall afresh on me (Iverson)

Blessing

God, the Creator, uphold you.
Christ, the Redeemer, enfold you.
The Holy Spirit, the Comforter, guide you,
and the blessing of God Almighty, the Father, the Son and the Holy Spirit be upon you and remain with you always.
Amen.

Celebrating the water made wine

Affirmation of God's presence

Affirmation

Today we celebrate the first miracle of Jesus at the wedding feast at Cana when he turned the water into wine. We celebrate the revealing of the power of Jesus to change our lives.

Invitation to worship

We rejoice in Christ's power to transform our lives and to fill our emptiness with the riches of his glory.
The Lord is here.
His Spirit is with us.

Hymn

New every morning is the love

Silence

Candle lighting

Have five people light the candles, speaking the sentences as they do so.

Holy God, holy and Strong One, in our emptiness we come to be filled by you. *(First candle is lit)*
The Lord is my light and my salvation.

Holy God, holy and Strong One, in our darkness we come to your light. *(Second candle is lit)*
The Lord is my light and my salvation.

Holy God, holy and Strong One, in our troubles we come to your love. *(Third candle is lit)*
The Lord is my light and my salvation.

Holy God, holy and Strong One, in illness we come for your healing.
(Fourth candle is lit)
The Lord is my light and my salvation.

Holy God, holy and Strong One, in need we come to your salvation.
(Fifth candle is lit)
The Lord is my light and my salvation.

Prayer

Lord you know our needs before we ask and are always more ready to give than we desire or deserve. We come to you for healing renewal and for the fullness of life eternal. Amen.

Silence

Ministry of the Word

Reading

1 Kings 17:8–16

Hymn

Jesus the Lord said, 'I am the bread'

The Gospel

John 2:1–11

Sermon

Silence

Hymn

Joy to the world

Response

Creed

Confession

Thanksgiving

Lord Jesus, we give thanks that you come to share in our joys and in our sorrows. We rejoice that you bring your strength to our weakness, your presence to our emptiness. We give thanks that in you we are transformed into your likeness and can share in your glory.

Intercessions

Lord, at the wedding of Cana,
you transformed common water into wine,
come and change us that we may know you and your love:
as you dear Lord have taken on our humanity
may we now partake of your Divinity.
Good Lord transform us
that we may reveal your glory.

Bless your Church as it seeks to reveal your glory in the world.
We remember especially all priests, pastors and ministers and all your faithful people in their obedience and witness to you.
We ask your blessing upon all that are preparing for marriage and all who are newly married. We pray for those saving to get married and all who feel that they cannot afford to marry.
Good Lord transform us
that we may reveal your glory.

Remember before you all that are discovering a newness in their love for each other.
We pray for marriages that have run into difficulties, for those who are running out of resources, those in debt and those having homes repossessed.
For all who feel betrayed in their love, for those seeking a divorce at this time.
We ask your blessing upon marriage guidance councils and all who seek to support family life.
Good Lord transform us
that we may reveal your glory.

Lord that your presence may transform our homes: that our homes may be centres of love, joy and peace.
We remember before you friends and loved ones and all who have transformed our lives by their goodness.
We ask that in our communities we may share and help to meet each other's needs.
We pray for those areas of darkness and deprivation within our communities.
Good Lord transform us
that we may reveal your glory.

We remember all who have run out of resources, the hungry and thirsty peoples of our world.
We ask your blessing upon the exhausted, the world-weary and all who can no longer cope on their own, upon all who are struggling to provide for their families and their basic needs.
We remember all who are in trouble or in sickness, especially . . .
Good Lord transform us
that we may reveal your glory.

We rejoice that in you the best is yet to come.
We give thanks for all who have entered into the glory of your kingdom.
We pray for loved ones departed from our sight, especially . . .
Merciful Father,
accept these prayers for the sake of your Son our Saviour Jesus Christ. Amen.

Collect

Almighty God,
whose Son revealed in signs and miracles
the wonder of your saving presence:
renew your people with your heavenly grace,
and in all our weakness
sustain us with your mighty power;
through Jesus Christ our Lord.
(Common Worship Collect for the Third Sunday of Epiphany)

The Lord's Prayer

Silence

Hymn

How sweet the name of Jesus sounds

Blessing

The love of the Lord Jesus fill you with joy and newness of life,
the Lord Jesus bring you to the fullness of his glory,
the Lord Jesus transform your days by his presence,
and the blessing of God Almighty, the Father, the Son and the Holy Spirit
be upon you and your loved ones now and always. Amen.

The mission of the Church

Affirmation of God's presence

Affirmation

God has called us to know him and to love him. Those whom God calls he sends. God wants to reveal himself to others through us and our way of life.

Invitation to worship

We are in the presence of God the Father, Son and Holy Spirit: we live in his light and are forever in his love. Come and give your love to him.

The Lord is here.
His Spirit is with us.

Hymn

I, the Lord of sea and sky

Silence

Candle lighting

Today we light our five candles to rejoice that Jesus is ever present and gives himself to us. He desires us to share in his love for the world.

Have five different people light the candles, speaking the sentences as they do so.

Jesus, Light of the World, I give myself to you. *(First candle is lit)*

Jesus, our loving Lord, I give myself to you. *(Second candle is lit)*

Jesus, our Friend and Saviour, I give myself to you. *(Third candle is lit)*

Jesus as you give yourself for us, I give myself to you. *(Fourth candle is lit)*

Jesus, the Son of God and Son of man, I give myself to you.
(Fifth candle is lit)

All **Jesus you call us to work with you: we give our lives to you.**

Prayer

Jesus Christ, Light of the World, you reveal yourself to your disciples. Open our ears to your call and help us to be faithful and serve you all our days. Amen.

Silence

Ministry of the Word

Reading

Isaiah 6:1–8

Hymn

We have a gospel to proclaim

The Gospel

Matthew 28:16–20

Sermon

Silence

Hymn

Firmly I believe and truly

Response

Creed

Confession

Thanksgiving

Blessed are you, Lord our God, for you have called us to know you and to abide with you. You have called us to love you and to tell of you. Blessed are you Father, Son and Holy Spirit for you have called us into life and life eternal. Blessed be God forever.

Intercessions

Father we ask your blessing upon the Church, that it may grow in love for you, that it may grow in holiness, that it may grow in size. We remember before you all who reach out in mission to tell of your love and your saving power. Lord guide all preachers of the word and teachers of the faith, all who witness by their daily lives and example. May we all share in bringing others to you and in revealing you to others.
Lord, as you call us,
fill us with your love.

Lord God, we pray for all who are being exploited by others. We remember the poor and the homeless and we ask your blessing upon all who are caring for refugees and deprived peoples. We pray for all who lack any moral or spiritual guidance and who are being led astray by people around them.
Lord, as you call us,
fill us with your love.

We give thanks for those who taught us the faith and who set us an example by their lives. We ask your blessing upon our homes, our loved ones and all who have cared for us. We pray for all who suffer from neglect, violence or a lack of love.
Lord, as you call us,
fill us with your love.

God, in you is our peace and our hope. We remember in your presence all ill and suffering people. We pray especially for any who feel confused by life and who are not able to cope. We pray for all who are caught

up in drug abuse or in vice. May all who deal with the troubled and distressed help to bring your peace and love to their lives.
Lord, as you call us,
fill us with your love.

We give thanks for your redeeming love and for the gift of life eternal. We ask your blessing on our loved ones departed and commend them, this world and ourselves to your unfailing love.
Merciful Father,
accept these prayers for the sake of your Son, our Saviour Jesus Christ. Amen.

Collect

God our creator,who in the beginning
commanded the light to shine out of darkness:
we pray that the light of the glorious gospel of Christ
may dispel the darkness of ignorance and unbelief,
shine into the hearts of all your people,
and reveal the knowledge of your glory
in the face of Jesus Christ your Son our Lord.

(Common Worship Collect for the Fourth Sunday of Epiphany)

The Lord's Prayer

Silence

Hymn

Forth in thy name, O Lord, I go

Blessing

The love of the Father empower you,
the light of the Saviour radiate from you,
the leading of the Spirit guide you
and the blessing of God Almighty, the Father, the Son and the Holy Spirit
be upon you now and for evermore. Amen.

Candlemas
The presentation of Christ in the Temple

Affirmation of God's presence

Affirmation

Today is the festival of the presentation of Christ in the Temple; it was known earlier as the festival of the purification of Mary. It is probably best known simply as Candlemas. There is a sense in which the lighting of the candles throughout the Advent, Christmas and Epiphany season now reach their climax. The forty days of Christmas close with Candlemas. The year is coming out of darkness and the days are lengthening. After today, we turn towards the season of Lent and look forward to Easter. As a symbol of this movement, we will process to the door of the church at the end of the service and there extinguish our candles.

It is our joy to welcome Christ as did Simeon and Anna: to welcome him as 'a light to lighten the nations of the world and the glory of his people Israel'. Let us rejoice in the Light of Christ that has come into our world.

Invitation to worship

We are in the light, the love and the glory of the Lord, Father, Son and Holy Spirit.

The Lord is here.
His Spirit is with us.

Hymn

Father, we adore you

Silence

Candle lighting

If possible have a candle for everyone to light during the service or at least one for a representative from each family.

Have five people come from different areas of the church for the candle lighting. Begin by telling the congregation the response to 'Christ as our Light,' is '**illumine and guide us**.'

As the five people light the candles each has a sentence to say:

Jesus Christ is the Light of all the peoples of world.
Christ as our Light,
illumine and guide us.

Jesus Christ is the Light that scatters the darkness.
Christ as our Light,
illumine and guide us.

Jesus Christ is the Light to show us the way to the Father.
Christ as our Light,
illumine and guide us.

Jesus Christ is the Light that leads us to eternal life.
Christ as our Light,
illumine and guide us.

The Good News is Jesus the Light of the World is with us now.
Christ as our Light,
illumine and guide us.

Hymn

We are marching in the light of God
(Let everyone receive a light from the main candles or from each other as the hymn is sung)

Prayer after the hymn

Blessed are you Lord our God for you have called us out of darkness to share in your light. The bright light of Christ scatters the darkness from within us and is a lantern to our path. Bless these lights that we

carry that they may remind us of your presence and of your saving love revealed through Christ our Lord.
Christ as our Light,
illumine and guide us.

Silence

Ministry of the Word

Reading

1 Samuel 1:20–28

Hymn

Christ is the world's light

The Gospel

Luke 2:22–40

Sermon

Silence

Hymn

Lord, the light of your love is shining

Response

Creed

Confession

Thanksgiving

Blessed are you Lord our God.
We give you thanks and praise for the creation of the light that gives life to the world.
We rejoice in Christ our Lord who brings light to our darkness.

We praise you for the light of Spirit, who inspires and guides us.
Today we give you thanks for the presentation of Christ in the Temple,
for the vision of Simeon,
for the faith of Anna,
for the steadfastness of Joseph,
for the courage of Mary, as she was told she would suffer with her Son.
Above all, we thank you that in Christ we triumph over darkness and death.
Blessed are you Father, Son and Holy Spirit, one God for ever and ever.
Amen.

Intercessions

By the mystery of the Word made flesh, Lord,
make yourself known to us.

By your coming as Christ the Light of the World, Lord,
make yourself known to us.

By your birth in Bethlehem, Lord,
make yourself known to us.

By your revealing to the shepherds and wise men, Lord,
make yourself known to us.

By your baptism, with the voice from the cloud and the descending dove, Lord,
make yourself known to us.

By your presence at the wedding at Cana and your changing water into wine, Lord,
make yourself known to us.

By your proclaiming of the Good News, Lord,
make yourself known to us.

God of light and love, we remember before you all who seek to proclaim the Good News. We ask your blessing upon all ministers of the word and the sacraments, upon all who teach and preach in your name. We pray for all who are striving to bring the Light of Christ to darkened lives.
Light of God,
shine upon us.

We remember all who live in darkness and in fear. We pray for the persecuted and the homeless, for all who are captives or suffer from war or terrorism. We ask your blessing upon all who are anxious for their lives.
Light of God,
shine upon us.

We remember for all who suffer from blindness or impairment of their sight. We ask you to bless all who seek to relieve their suffering and to restore sight. We pray for any who have lost vision of you and your love.
Light of God,
shine upon us.

We remember all who are in the valley of the shadow of death and all who have passed beyond it to light and life eternal. We pray for our loved ones departed from us. May we all come to rejoice in the fullness of your kingdom.
Merciful Father,
accept these prayers for the sake of your Son, our Saviour Jesus Christ.
Amen.

Collect

Almighty Father,
whose Son Jesus Christ was presented in the Temple
and acclaimed the glory of Israel
and the light of the nations:
grant that in him we may be presented to you
and in the world may reflect his glory:
through Jesus Christ our Lord,
who is alive and reigns with you and the Holy Spirit,
one God, now and for ever.
Amen.
(The Alternative Service Book 1980)

The Lord's Prayer

Silence

Hymn

The Nunc dimittis *or* Faithful vigil ended
(During the hymn there is a procession to the door)

Here we turn from our celebration of Christ's coming into the world and towards Lent and Easter: turning from his birth to his passion and resurrection. We remember that he came among us and that he shares in our joys and sorrows. May we, who now extinguish these candles, let the light of Christ shine in our hearts and lives and bring his light to the world. *(The candles are extinguished)*

Blessing

The Lord Jesus, give light to your eyes,
give light to your mind,
give light to your heart,
give light to your hands,
give light to your whole life,
that you may witness to him and live for him, today and forever,
and the blessing of God Almighty, the Father, the Son and the Holy Spirit be upon you and remain with you always.
Amen.

You'll also enjoy:

Looking and Longing
1500634

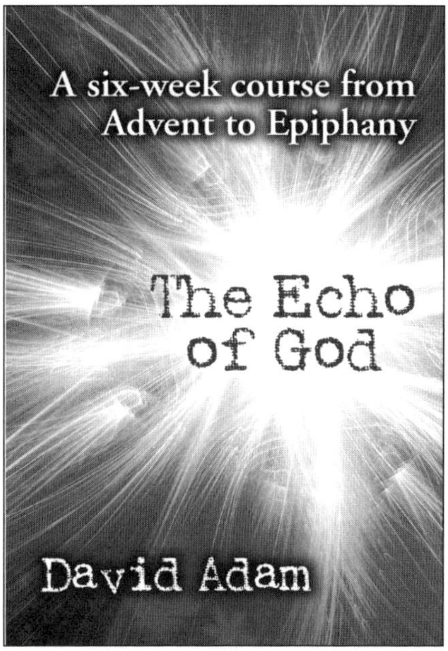

The Echo of God
1501113

A Prayer a Day
1501112

Candles in the Dark
Book 1500718
CD 1490151